# THE ANCIENT INCAS

BY MADELINE TYLER

**KidHaven**
PUBLISHING

UNLOCKING ANCIENT CIVILIZATIONS

Published in 2019 by KidHaven Publishing, an Imprint of Greenhaven Publishing, LLC
353 3rd Avenue, Suite 255, New York, NY 10010

Written by: Madeline Tyler
Edited by: John Wood
Designed by: Daniel Scase

Cataloging-in-Publication Data

Names: Tyler, Madeline.
Title: The ancient Incas / Madeline Tyler.
Description: New York : KidHaven Publishing, 2019. | Series: Unlocking ancient civilizations | Includes glossary and index.
Identifiers: ISBN 9781534529076 (pbk.) | ISBN 9781534529090 (library bound) | ISBN 9781534529083 (6 pack) |
ISBN 9781534529106 (ebook)
Subjects: LCSH: Incas--Juvenile literature. | Incas--History--Juvenile literature. | Incas--Social life and customs--Juvenile literature.
Classification: LCC F3429.T95 2019 | DDC 985'.01--dc23

Printed in the United States of America

CPSIA compliance information: Batch # BW19KL: For further information
contact Greenhaven Publishing LLC, New York, New York at 1-844-317-7404.

# PHOTO CREDITS

# THE ANCIENT INCAS

## CONTENTS

Words that look like *this* are explained in the glossary on page 31.

# THE ANCIENT INCAS

THE Inca were a group of people that lived in the Andes mountains in Peru from around **A.D.** 1100 until 1572. The Inca began as a small *tribe* but soon grew into a large, organized *civilization*. The Inca society was so successful that, in around A.D. 1500, they were in control of the biggest *empire* in the world. The Inca Empire stretched 2,175 miles (3,500 km) from present-day Ecuador in the north, and south through Peru, Bolivia, Chile, and Argentina.

The Andes are made up of several mountain ranges that can be found along the western coast of South America. They are the longest chain of mountains in the world and have the highest peaks in North, South, and Central America. There are many earthquakes and volcanic eruptions in this area.

RAINFORESTS, SNOW, AND GRASSLANDS CAN ALL BE FOUND IN THE ANDES.

# THE BEGINNINGS OF THE ANCIENT INCA

Before the Inca Empire began, the Inca were a small group of traveling people who had no permanent home. They were **nomadic** and moved across the Andes to find new **settlements** all the time. Inca legend says that their first leader, Manco Capac, settled in Cuzco with his followers in around A.D. 1200. Cuzco is a city in Urubamba Valley, an area between the mountains in the Andes of Peru.

MANCO CAPAC

Urubamba Valley is sometimes called the Sacred Valley of the Incas and is home to many ancient ruins from the Inca Empire. Urubamba Valley has very **fertile** farming land and is surrounded by many rivers that provided the Incas with water.

# BEFORE THE INCAS

THESE NAZCA LINES MAKE THE SHAPE OF A MONKEY. OTHER SHAPES INCLUDE A SPIDER, A DOG, A TREE, AND A WHALE.

**H**UNDREDS of years before the Inca Empire, a civilization called the Nazca was developing on the southern coast of Peru. The Nazca existed between 200 **B.C.** and A.D. 600 and lived in many areas that were eventually taken over by the Incas. The Nazca created giant patterns in the desert by scraping stones and earth away. These lines, which can still be seen today, are known as the "Nazca Lines" and no one is completely sure why they were drawn. Some historians believe that they have something to do with *astronomy*. Others have suggested that the Nazca may have used them in a ritual to pray to the gods for water, as this area is very dry and is difficult to grow crops in.

AFTER A LONG *drought* THAT LASTED FOR 30 YEARS, THE NAZCA WERE DEFEATED BY ANOTHER CIVILIZATION CALLED THE WARI.

HUMMINGBIRD

HUNDREDS of years later, and many miles away on the northern coast of Peru, a civilization called the Chimú was growing into the largest empire of the time. The Chimú people lived between the 12th century and 15th century A.D. and were very advanced.

In around A.D. 1470, an Inca leader called Tupac Yupanqui captured the Chimú leader, Minchançaman, and kept him prisoner. The Incas invaded the Chimú capital city, Chan Chan, and took control of the Chimú civilization.

ALTHOUGH THE INCAS TOOK CONTROL OF THE CHIMÚ AND BECAME A MUCH LARGER EMPIRE, CHAN CHAN IS STILL THE LARGEST EVER CITY OF *pre-Columbian* AMERICA.

When the Chimú people became part of the Inca Empire, the Incas were very inspired by Chimú art, politics, and architecture. The Incas loved Chimú art so much that they made thousands of Chimú artists move to Cuzco so that they could create sculptures, pottery, and other pieces of art for the Inca rulers.

# THE INCA EMPIRE

## THE KINGDOM OF CUZCO

**D**URING the first few years of the Inca civilization, the Incas were settled in Cuzco and did not explore very far. Cuzco was surrounded by fertile lands and sources of water, so they had no need to expand their empire.

However, by the 14th century, Cuzco was not getting enough rain to water all their crops. The Inca's fourth leader, Mayta Capac, helped the kingdom to spread by battling other people that lived in the valley and taking their homes.

In A.D. 1425, the eighth Sapa Inca, or Supreme Inca, Viracocha Inca, began to build up the kingdom even more and at a much faster rate. He led his people into war and defeated enemy kingdoms to *conquer* new lands. Viracocha Inca placed Inca leaders in charge of these places to stop any *rebellions*.

# THE RISE OF THE INCA EMPIRE

As more lands were conquered by the Incas, the Kingdom of Cuzco soon became the Inca Empire. Viracocha Inca's son, Pachacuti Inca Yupanqui, ruled the Inca Empire from A.D. 1438 until 1471. Pachacuti Inca Yupanqui rebuilt Cuzco and transformed it into a grand capital city. He created an Inca religion, built temples, and constructed *terraces* on the sides of the mountains where crops could be grown (see page 16). He also founded the city of Machu Picchu, conquered the Chimú people, and claimed their city Chan Chan.

TERRACES

MACHU PICCHU

THE INCA EMPIRE STRETCHED SO FAR THAT IT EVENTUALLY BECAME KNOWN AS TAHUANTINSUYU, OR "LAND OF THE FOUR QUARTERS".

Pachacuti Inca Yupanqui's son, Tupac Inca Yupanqui, was one of the most successful Inca emperors. He was in charge between 1471 and 1493 and, during his reign, he expanded the empire and took control of areas in present-day Chile. Tupac Inca Yupanqui doubled the size of the Inca Empire by the time his son, Huayna Capac, became emperor. Huayna Capac continued his father's success by extending the empire into the north and building roads and cities throughout the area.

# CITIES OF THE INCA

NCA cities were high up in the Andes mountains. Often, they all had a similar layout with a palace, a kallanka, a kancha, and a qollqa.

- A kallanka is a large building that was used for large community gatherings and as somewhere for important members of the Inca *government* to stay in.
- A kancha is a group of three or more buildings that are arranged around a courtyard. Kanchas were mostly used as government buildings and temples.
- Qollqas are storehouses. The Incas kept foods such as grain and potatoes in the qollqas and they stayed fresh for around two years.

Earthquakes are very common in the Andes. The Incas had to build their cities so that they would not collapse when an earthquake hit. They did this by carefully cutting stone blocks so that they could fit together exactly. This method made the structures strong enough to withstand many earthquakes without being damaged.

QOLLQA RUINS

One of the most well-known ancient Inca cities is Machu Picchu, in present-day Peru. Machu Picchu was hidden in the Andes for hundreds of years until it was rediscovered in 1911 by an explorer named Hiram Bingham.

THE SACRED ROCK, OR THE TEMPLE OF THE SUN, IS AN IMPORTANT BUILDING IN MACHU PICCHU. THE INCAS USED IT AS A PLACE TO WORSHIP THE SUN GOD, INTI.

Machu Picchu was built around A.D. 1450 by Pachacuti Inca Yupanqui and is named after one of the two mountain peaks that it sits between: Machu Picchu and Huayna Picchu. Many historians believe that Machu Picchu was built as a royal city for Pachacuti Inca Yupanqui and his family to live in. Some people think it was built as somewhere that the Sapa Inca could go on holiday to, while others believe it was a religious city. As well as the royal family, Machu Picchu was large enough for up to 1,000 people to live in.

# ROADS

The Incas built roads that covered over 24,850 miles (40,000 km) of their empire. The roads ran through mountains and deserts, and along the coast. The roads connected major Inca cities and helped them with travel and trade. The Inca road system, or Qhapaq Ñan, had four main routes which all started in Cuzco, at the center of the four quarters of the Inca Empire.

The Incas took a long time to make sure their roads were well built and of a high standard. This was because Qhapaq Ñan was seen as a symbol of the empire and was often the first thing that people saw of the Inca civilization. They wanted to show prisoners, merchants, and other traveling people how advanced their empire was and how skillful their people were.

SOME ROADS WERE BUILT UP TO 16,400 FEET (5,000 M) HIGH ALONG THE EDGES OF MOUNTAINS. IMPORTANT ROADS HAD STONES ARRANGED ON TOP OF THEM TO MAKE THEM SMOOTHER AND EASIER TO TRAVEL ON.

Bridges also made up Qhapaq Ñan, and linked parts of the route that were blocked by rivers or sections of mountain. The bridges were made of stone, or grass, and reeds. They were checked regularly by the Suyuyuq, the official Inca bridge inspector, to see if they needed repairing or replacing. However, it was the responsibility of the local people to make these repairs. They saw it as part of their duty to the empire.

The Incas made rope bridges by twisting dried grass together to make ropes. Queshuachaca is an Inca rope bridge that is 148 feet (45 m) long and crosses the Apurimac River. It is the oldest surviving Inca rope bridge and is still repaired every year by Inca people who live nearby.

QUESHUACHACA

The Inca Bridge crosses a 20-foot (6 m) gap in a stone path that leads to Machu Picchu. The bridge was originally made from tree trunks that could easily be lifted up if the Incas wanted to make it harder for people to reach Machu Picchu.

THE INCA BRIDGE

# EVERYDAY LIFE

## INCA SOCIETY

INCA society was organized in a **hierarchy**. The Sapa Inca, or Emperor, was at the top and ruled the whole of the Inca Empire. He wore the finest clothes and ate his food from plates made of gold. He was worshipped like a god and was carried everywhere by servants. Many officials and noblemen helped the Sapa Inca to rule, including the governors of each quarter of Tahuantinsuyu. The commoners and **peasants** were at the bottom of society. They were often poor and worked as farmers.

Inca peasants had to pay **taxes** to the Emperor. These taxes were called mit'a and the Incas paid them by farming and growing crops; building roads, temples, and bridges; and serving as soldiers or messengers. In exchange for paying their taxes, the government gave the peasants food and clothing.

Inca society was divided further into ayllus. Ayllus were made up of peasant families that lived near each other in the same village. Some ayllus owned a piece of land where they could grow crops to feed the empire. Other ayllus made clothing, jewelry, or pottery.

INCA FAMILIES LIVED TOGETHER IN RECTANGULAR HOUSES THAT ONLY HAD ONE ROOM. INCA PEASANT HOUSES DID NOT HAVE ANY FURNITURE. PEOPLE SAT AND SLEPT ON BLANKETS AND CARPETS.

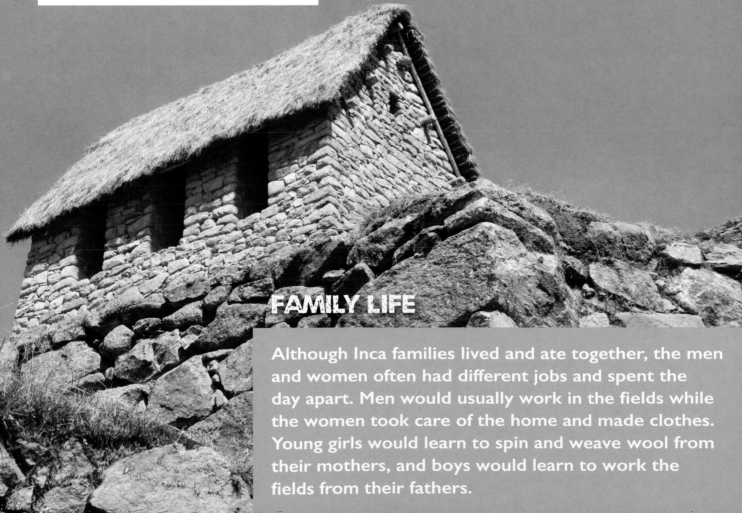

## FAMILY LIFE

Although Inca families lived and ate together, the men and women often had different jobs and spent the day apart. Men would usually work in the fields while the women took care of the home and made clothes. Young girls would learn to spin and weave wool from their mothers, and boys would learn to work the fields from their fathers.

# FARMING

## AGRICULTURE

**A**GRICULTURE is another word for farming, and it was very important to the Inca Empire. They grew **quinoa** (say: keen-wa) and potatoes high up in the mountains, maize in the valleys, and tomatoes, peppers, beans, and fruits on the lowlands. These could either be eaten or traded for other goods.

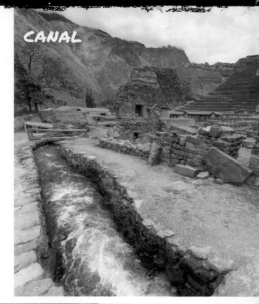
CANAL

TERRACING

Farming was often difficult because the land was very uneven. Some areas of land were too dry to grow crops, while others were too wet. To solve these problems, the Incas built terraces, *canals*, and *irrigation* and drainage networks: wetlands were drained, and irrigation canals watered dry areas.

The Incas cut large steps into the mountainsides to create flat land so that they could plant crops. These steps are called terraces and they allowed the Incas to farm on the steep mountains. Instead of flowing straight down the mountain, rainwater can stop at each new step because they are flat. This made sure that nowhere got too wet or too dry.

# ANIMALS

The Incas **domesticated** animals such as llamas and alpacas. They were important to Inca life and provided the people with meat, wool, and leather. The Incas often bred llamas to use them as pack animals to carry heavy loads along the Qhapaq Ñan to different cities and villages. Llamas are much stronger than humans, so they could carry large amounts of food, textiles, and building materials across long distances.

Alpacas are smaller than llamas and are not as strong. Instead of being used as pack animals, the Incas bred alpacas for their soft fleece. Women used alpaca and llama fleece to spin wool. They used the alpaca and llama wool to weave clothing and blankets. The softest cloth was decorated with gold and silver and was given to the Emperor.

# RELIGION

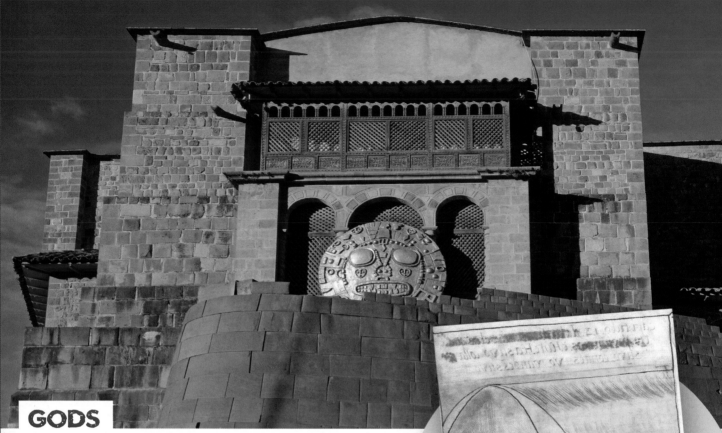

## GODS

**T**HE Incas worshipped many gods, but the most important was Inti, the Sun god. Inti was at the center of Inca religion and was celebrated in festivals and rituals. Honoring Inti, and the other Inca gods, was an important part of Inca life and one way they did this was by building large temples. One of the holiest temples of the Inca Empire was Coricancha, or Qorikancha, in Cuzco. Coricancha is also called the Temple of the Sun and was dedicated to the Sun god Inti. The temple was built by Pachacuti Inca Yupanqui between A.D. 1438 and 1471 and was once covered in gold and jewels. However, Spanish invaders stole this gold in the 15th and 16th centuries, and there are now only a few stone walls of the temple left.

**INTI WAS OFTEN DRAWN AS A BRIGHT YELLOW OR GOLDEN SUN WITH LOTS OF RAYS.**

Inca religion was focused on the natural world, and their gods often represented parts of nature. Mama Quilla was the goddess of the Moon, Pachamama was the goddess of the Earth, Apu Illapu was the god of rain, and Viracocha was the god of creation.

The Incas held many ceremonies and rituals at their temples. They were usually led by religious leaders called priests. The High Priest was the most important priest in the Inca Empire. He was often the emperor's brother and lived in Cuzco.

Inca festivals involved music, dancing, and feasts. Sometimes, they would also require a sacrifice. This is when a person or animal is killed during a special ceremony to please and honor the gods. The Incas were taught that their emperor was a **descendant** of Inti and should be treated like a god. They believed that giving sacrifices to the gods would keep the Sapa Inca healthy. During a special festival called the Inti Raymi, the High Priest performed sacrifices using a knife called a tumi. Tumi knives usually had a semicircular blade and were decorated with jewels. They were made from gold, silver, bronze, or copper and had the face of a person on the handle.

TUMI

INTI RAYMI IS STILL CELEBRATED BY *indigenous* PEOPLE LIVING IN THE ANDES MOUNTAINS.

# THE CREATION STORY

**M**OST religions have a story that explains how the gods made the Earth, the sea, humans, plants, and animals. This is called the creation story, or the creation myth, and it is different for every religion.

VIRACOCHA

The Incas believed that Viracocha, the god of creation, came out of Lake Titicaca in Peru and created the land and sky. According to the Inca tradition, he also created people that were similar to giants. The giants made Viracocha angry so, to punish them, he flooded the land until they all died. After this, Viracocha made humans and gave them the Sun, Moon, and stars so that they could live in light. Viracocha traveled round the world to give his people language, clothing, arts, and agriculture. The Incas believed that Viracocha would one day return to them.

THE RUINS OF THE TEMPLE OF VIRACOCHA ARE A POPULAR TOURIST DESTINATION IN PERU.

# INCA AFTERLIFE

If the Incas led a good life, they believed they would go to Hanan Pacha when they died. Hanan Pacha was the Inca paradise and was where Inti and Mama Quilla could be found. However, if they behaved very badly, the Incas believed they would be sent to the underworld, which was called Uku Pacha. Uku Pacha was underneath Earth and was ruled by Supay, the Inca god of death.

THE MUMMIES OF INCA PEASANTS WERE KEPT IN CAVES OR TOMBS. ROYAL INCA MUMMIES HAD A SPECIAL ROOM IN THEIR PALACE WHERE THEY WERE KEPT WITH THEIR WIVES.

## BURIAL CUSTOMS

When Incas died, they were mummified. This means that the insides of the body were removed, and the body was then wrapped in several layers of cloth. The mummies were very important to the Incas and they saw the mummies as being a link to the gods. Inca mummies were often treated like living people. They were brought to ceremonies like weddings or harvests and were offered food and drink. Royal mummies were worshipped and still owned all of the land and possessions that they had owned when they were alive.

# ART AND CULTURE

The Incas made art from many different materials. They weaved and embroidered cloth, made pottery and ceramics, and created jewelry using gold, silver, and precious stones like turquoise. Many pieces of Inca art, like gold decoration in temples, were made to honor the gods. The Incas believed that gold was the sweat of Inti, and that silver was the tears of Quilla, the goddess of the Moon.

CONOPA

Most Inca pottery was practical and served a purpose. They made many pots that could be used to store water or foods such as maize, as well as serving plates, vases, and bowls. Some ceramics, like conopas, were made to be used in religious rituals. Conopas were often made in the shape of a llama or alpaca and were used to bring *fertility* to an Inca peasant's herd of animals.

# QUIPU

The ancient Incas did not have an alphabet or a writing system. This made recording important information very difficult and meant that they had to find a different way of remembering things like dates, names, or numbers.

QUIPU

Quipu are a system of knots that the Incas used instead of a written language. They were made of different colored strings with knots tied at different positions on the strings. The type of knot, its position on the string, and the number of knots all represented something different. The Incas used quipu to store information and records of the population, herds, weapons, and goods. Quipu were "read" by official experts, called quipucamayocs. They were also used by chasquis, Inca messengers, who traveled with the quipu to different cities and villages.

# THE END OF THE ANCIENT INCAS

**W**HEN the Inca Empire was at its largest, it covered about 3,400 miles (5,500 km) from Colombia to Argentina, and had a population of over ten million people. Because the empire was so big, it was often difficult to control. In the 16th century, the Inca Empire was beginning to collapse. There were many rebellions where different Incas would call themselves the new Sapa Inca and make a new capital city. This made the empire very weak and led to *civil war*.

THE EXECUTION OF THE INCA.

THIS DRAWING BY FELIPE GUAMÁN POMA DE AYALA SHOWS THE FIRST TIME THAT FRANCISCO PIZARRO MET WITH THE INCA EMPEROR, ATAHUALPA.

In 1492, Italian explorer Christopher Columbus led a voyage that sailed to the Americas. This was the first time that people from Europe had seen these places and the people that lived there. Forty years later, in 1532, a Spanish man named Francisco Pizarro arrived in South America. The Spanish invaders wanted to *colonize* the area and take control of the land and the Inca people, including the Sapa Inca, Atahualpa.

In November 1532, Pizarro led an attack against Atahualpa and his people in Cajamarca, a city in Peru. This was called the Battle of Cajamarca and was over very quickly. All 128 of the Spanish invaders survived the battle, but around 7,000 Incas were killed. They captured Atahualpa and took him prisoner, eventually killing him in July 1533. Although the Incas had a much larger army, the Spanish had horses, armor, guns, and swords. This gave the Spanish a huge advantage over the Incas.

ATAHUALPA

When the Spanish **colonizers** arrived in Central America, they brought many European diseases to the indigenous people, such as smallpox. Smallpox soon spread from Central America to the Inca Empire in South America.

After they had already become weak from war, many Incas died from these diseases. Historians believe that between 65% and 90% of the Inca population died from smallpox.

# THE LEGACY OF THE

## FREEZE-DRYING

**A**LTHOUGH the Spanish invaders destroyed many of the Incas' buildings, sculptures, and works of art, some parts of their culture and civilization can still be seen today. From the ancient ruins of Machu Picchu, to the information stored on the quipu, the Incas' **legacy** is still present today.

ASTRONAUTS TAKE FREEZE-DRIED FOOD, LIKE FREEZE-DRIED ICE-CREAM, TO SPACE. THIS IS BECAUSE IT CAN LAST FOR A VERY LONG TIME AND IT IS VERY LIGHT TO CARRY.

Freeze-drying is a way of storing food that makes it last for a long time. To freeze-dry something, you first remove all the water and then freeze the food at a very cold temperature. The Incas stored food like potatoes at very high *altitudes* in the Andes mountains. The high altitudes caused the water inside the potatoes to turn into *vapor* and the cold temperature on the mountain made the food freeze. They could then be kept for a long time without going rotten or moldy.

# ANCIENT INCAS

## GOLD JEWELRY

Gold jewelry is popular all around the world, but the Incas were some of the first people to make and wear it. Gold is a metal that is found underground as small nuggets and is mined to be turned into things like rings, necklaces, and crowns. Gold was very common in the Americas during this time.

Although gold was common, it was still very precious to the Incas. They used it to decorate their temples, to make religious objects used in rituals, and as jewelry worn by Inca royalty. In the Inca Empire, wearing gold jewelry showed that a person was powerful and wealthy. Miniature sculptures of llamas were made from gold and were presented to the gods as an *offering* during religious ceremonies where an animal was sacrificed. Gold was very *sacred* and was often associated with the god Inti, so people were usually buried in their tomb with all their gold possessions.

# TIMELINE OF THE

## A.D. 600
> END OF THE NAZCA CIVILIZATION

## A.D. 1100
> START OF THE INCA EMPIRE

## A.D. 1200
> MANCO CAPAC SETTLES IN CUZCO

## A.D. 1425
> VIRACOCHA INCA BUILDS UP THE INCA EMPIRE

## A.D. 1471-1493
> TUPAC INCA YUPANQUI RULES THE INCA EMPIRE

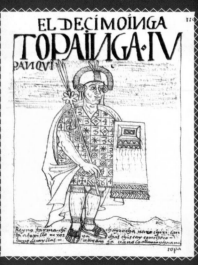

## A.D. 1500
> THE INCA HAVE THE LARGEST EMPIRE IN THE WORLD

## A.D. 1532
> FRANCISCO PIZARRO REACHES SOUTH AMERICA

# ANCIENT INCAS

## A.D. 1438-1471

→

PACHACUTI INCA YUPANQUI RULES THE INCA EMPIRE

## A.D. 1450

→

MACHU PICCHU IS BUILT

## A.D. 1470

→

CHIMÚ LEADER MINCHANÇAMAN IS CAPTURED BY THE INCA, WHICH BRINGS AN END TO THE CHIMÚ CIVILIZATION

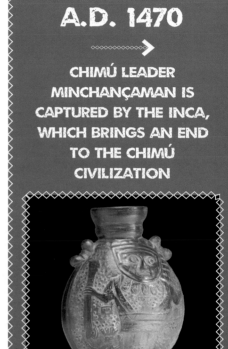

## A.D. NOVEMBER 1532

→

7,000 INCAS ARE KILLED IN THE BATTLE OF CAJAMARCA

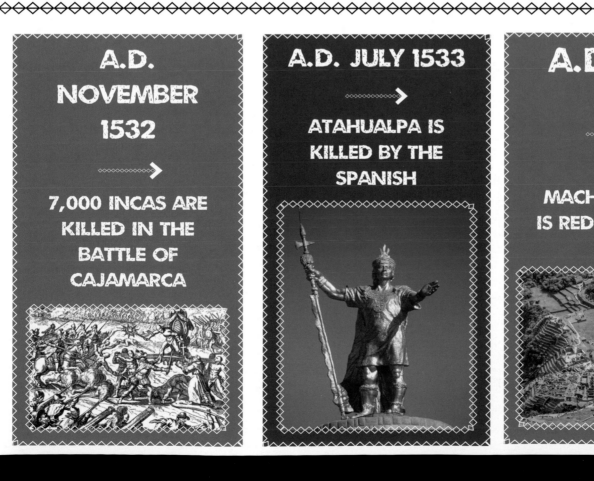

## A.D. JULY 1533

→

ATAHUALPA IS KILLED BY THE SPANISH

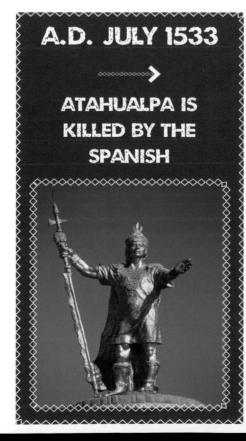

## A.D. 1911

→

MACHU PICCHU IS REDISCOVERED

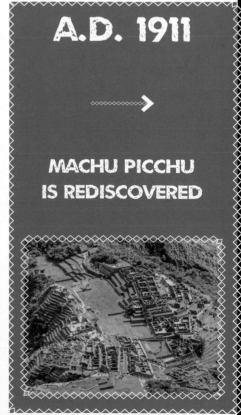

# MAP OF THE ANCIENT INCAS

COLOMBIA

ECUADOR

PERU

CAJAMARCA

MACHU PICCHU

CUZCO

BRAZIL

LAKE TITICACA

BOLIVIA

ROADS

ARGENTINA

CHILE

# GLOSSARY

| | |
|---|---|
| A.D. | "in the year of the Lord", marks the time after Christians believe Jesus was born |
| altitudes | the heights of objects in relation to sea level or ground level |
| astronomy | the study of planets, stars, and the universe |
| B.C. | meaning"'before Christ", it is used to mark dates that occurred before Christians believe Jesus was born |
| canals | a human-made channel of water, similar to a river |
| civil war | fighting between different groups of people in the same country |
| civilization | a society that is very advanced |
| colonize | to move to a new land in order to take control of the area and people |
| colonizers | people that move to a new land to take control of the area and people |
| conquer | to overcome or take control of something by force |
| descendant | someone who comes after another person, or a group of people, in a family line |
| domesticated | tamed an animal so that it can be kept by humans |
| drought | a long period of very little rainfall, which leads to a lack of water |
| empire | a group of countries or nations under one ruler |
| fertile | soil that is able to grow strong, healthy crops |
| fertility | the ability to have offspring |
| government | the group of people with the authority to run a country and decide its laws |
| hierarchy | a system where people are ranked in order of power, status, or authority |
| indigenous | originating or naturally found in a particular place |
| irrigation | human-made systems that add water to crops at regular intervals |
| legacy | something handed down from one generation to the next |
| nomadic | not living in one permanent place |
| offering | a sacred and religious gift |
| peasants | poor land workers who belonged to the lowest social class |
| pre-Columbian | existing or happening in the Americas before the arrival of Christopher Columbus |
| quinoa | a plant that grows in the Andes whose seeds can be used like grain |
| rebellions | times when people fight against their government, leader, or ruler |
| sacred | connected to a god or gods |
| settlements | places where people choose to live and build communities in the form of villages or towns |
| taxes | payments made to the government so that they can provide services |
| terraces | flat, raised sections of ground |
| tribe | a group of people linked together by family, society, religion, or community |
| vapor | a substance in the gaseous state |

# INDEX